Photosynthesis

BY MARTHA LONDON

CONTENT CONSULTANT
WILLIAM W. ADAMS III, PhD
PROFESSOR, ECOLOGY AND EVOLUTIONARY BIOLOGY
UNIVERSITY OF COLORADO BOULDER

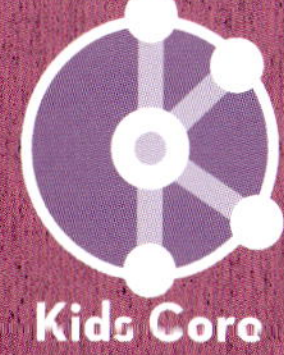

Kids Core
An Imprint of Abdo Publishing
abdobooks.com

abdobooks.com

Published by Abdo Publishing, a division of ABDO, PO Box 398166, Minneapolis, Minnesota 55439.

Printed in the United States of America, North Mankato, Minnesota
052021
092021

Cover Photo: Romolo Tavani/Shutterstock Images
Interior Photos: Brandt Bolding/iStockphoto, 4–5; Janette Hall/iStockphoto, 6; SJ Travel Photo and Video/Shutterstock Images, 8; Anna Om/iStockphoto, 10–11; Christopher Meade/Shutterstock Images, 12; Doug Dolde/iStockphoto, 13; Thomas Vogel/iStockphoto, 15; Shutterstock Images, 16, 21, 29; N. Nehring/iStockphoto, 18–19; Vitalii Dumma/iStockphoto, 22; Tracie Louise/iStockphoto, 23; Power and Syred/Science Source, 24; iStockphoto, 25; Cheryl Ramalho/iStockphoto, 26

Editor: Marie Pearson
Series Designer: Katharine Hale

Library of Congress Control Number: 2020948338

Publisher's Cataloging-in-Publication Data

Names: London, Martha, author.
Title: Photosynthesis / by Martha London
Description: Minneapolis, Minnesota : Abdo Publishing, 2022 | Series: Discover biology | Includes online resources and index.
Identifiers: ISBN 9781532195341 (lib. bdg.) | ISBN 9781098215651 (ebook)
Subjects: LCSH: Biology--Juvenile literature. | Photosynthesis--Juvenile literature. | Plant physiology--Juvenile literature. | Botany--Juvenile literature.
Classification: DDC 571.2--dc23

CONTENTS

Daffodils can start growing in early spring.

CHAPTER 1

Flowers Growing

Molly and her family walked through the garden in early spring. Green daffodil leaves were sprouting. Daffodils were a sign winter was over. The leaves got bigger as the weather got warmer. Sunlight shone on the leaves.

Daffodils are one of many plants that use photosynthesis to make food.

Molly asked her mom why the daffodil had leaves. Her mom explained that the leaves took in sunlight. They used the sunlight to make energy for the plant. This process is called photosynthesis.

A shoot poked out from the middle of the daffodil. It grew straight toward the sky. Molly measured the shoot as it grew taller. Soon, the head of a flower appeared on top of the shoot. In a couple of days, all of the yellow daffodil flowers were blooming. Grass grew around the daffodils. Sunlight provided energy for all these plants to grow.

Different Plants, Different Needs

Some plants need a lot of sunlight. Others do better in the shade. Each type of plant is **adapted** to the places where it naturally grows. Plants that do best in shade may get burnt in full sunlight. Plants that need a lot of sun do not get enough energy in the shade.

Leaves often have a broad shape to help them catch sunlight.

What Is Photosynthesis?

Plants use photosynthesis to get energy. Plants use the energy to live and grow. Photosynthesis is a process with many steps. It happens in plant **cells**. Cells are the smallest living units in plants and animals. For a plant to get bigger, cells need to form more cells. They can only do this with energy from sugars.

Explore Online

Visit the website below. Does it give any new information about how plants grow that wasn't in Chapter One?

How Do Seeds Sprout?

abdocorelibrary.com/photosynthesis

Some trees have leaves that do not fall off in winter. But they usually do not photosynthesize when it's cold.

CHAPTER 2

Cells at Work

Photosynthesis happens in a plant's cells. Cells have many jobs. Plants' cells help support them. A stiff cell wall surrounds each plant cell. The collective strength of many connected cell walls helps hold the plant upright.

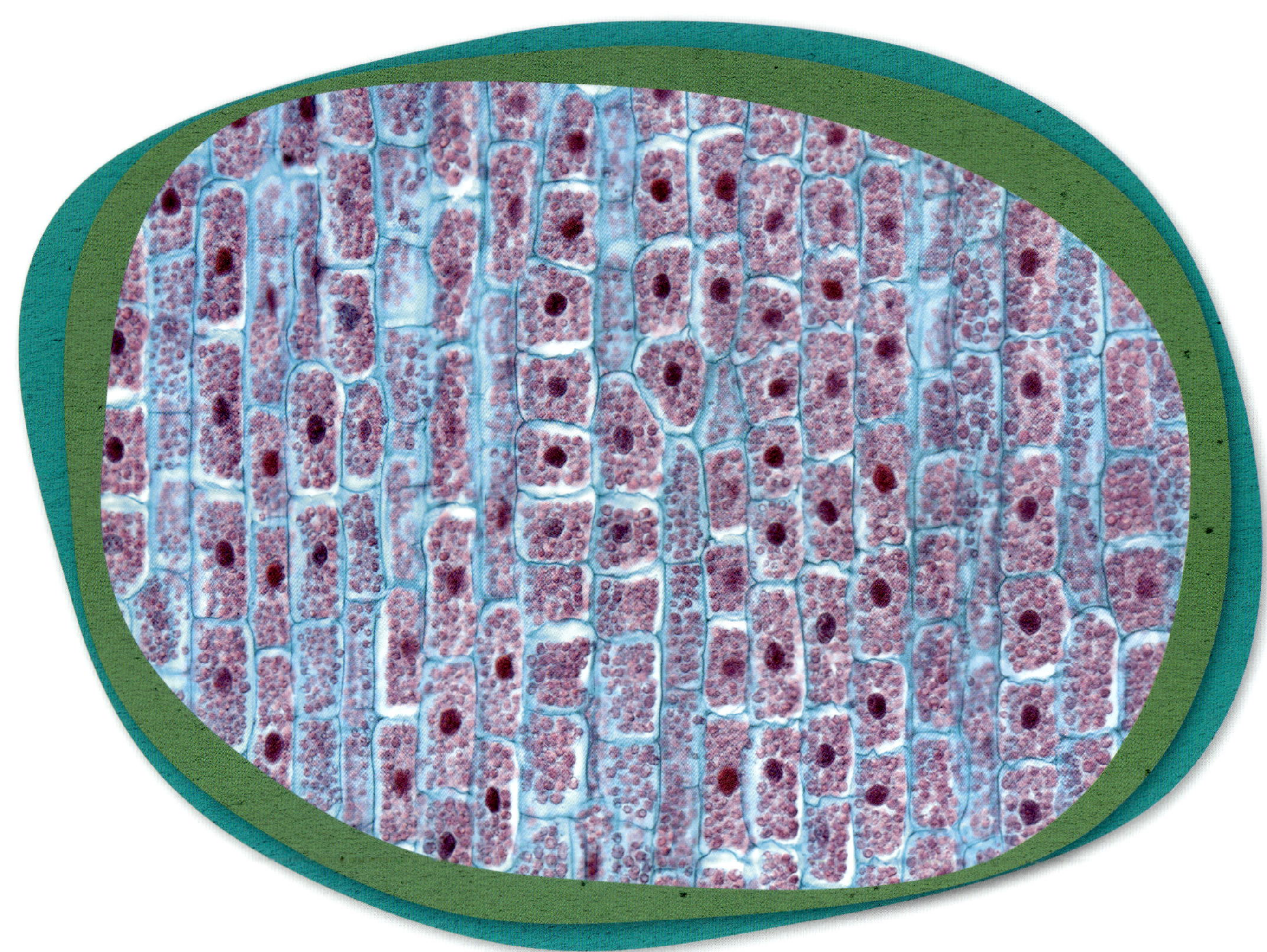

Cell walls, *blue lines*, help plant cells stack up and give the plant its shape.

Photosynthesis Ingredients

Cells also provide energy for the plant or animal. Plants and animals get energy in different ways. Animals get energy from what

A plant's cells help it stand tall.

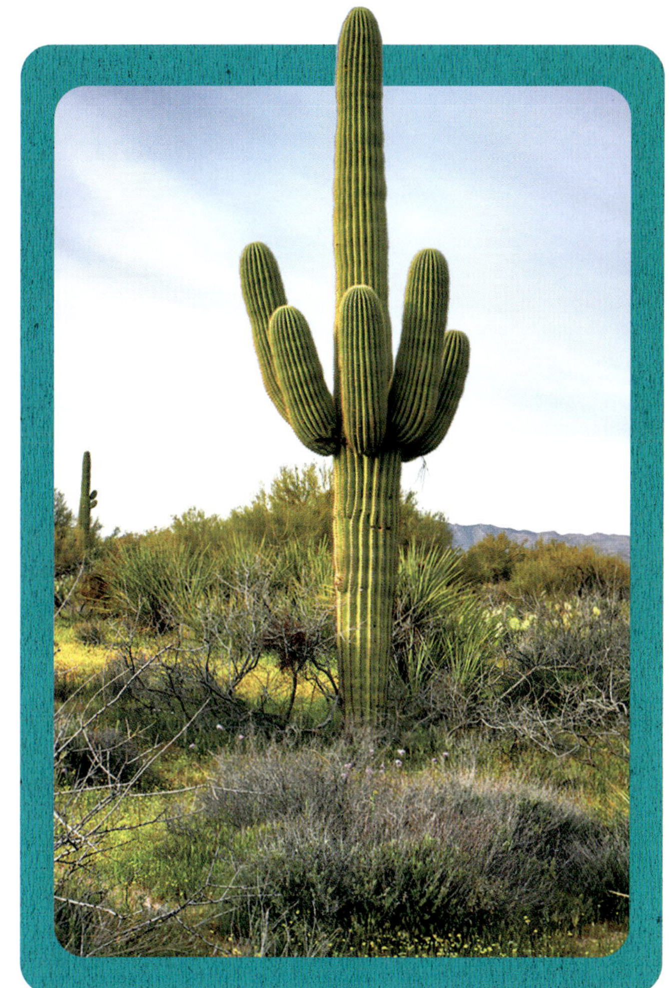

they eat. Most plants do not eat other plants or animals. Instead, plants take in **nutrients** from the air and water to get energy.

Plants use three ingredients to make energy-rich sugars. The ingredients are sunlight, carbon dioxide, and water.

The sun gives off light. Light is a form of energy. Sunlight shines on a plant's leaves. The leaves capture that energy. Carbon dioxide is a gas in the air. It moves into a plant's leaves through tiny openings called stomata during photosynthesis. Many plants have roots that

Something in the Soil

Many plants need soil in order to grow. Soil allows water to trickle down to plant roots. But soil can become pressed together and hardened. Hard soil is not as good for plants. Less water soaks in. Plant roots cannot spread as easily through the soil. Plants cannot get the water they need to grow. Soil that is too loose cannot hold water. Plants in this type of soil need frequent watering.

Plants use their leaves and roots to get what they need to make sugars.

take in water from the soil. Water has nutrients that plants need to be healthy. Water travels up the roots and into cells in the leaves.

Veins carry water from the roots to the leaves. They also carry sugars from the leaves to the rest of thc plant.

All three of these ingredients are used during photosynthesis. They make energy-rich sugars. Plants turn sunlight, water, and carbon dioxide into energy that the plants can use.

Primary Source

Alessia Para Gallio studies plants. She explained in an interview how plants help clean the air:

> Carbon dioxide is one of the major air pollutants, so [plants] are actually keeping the air clean. In the process, they produce oxygen, which [makes up a big] portion of the air we breathe.

Source: Bethany Hubbard. "The Power of Photosynthesis." *Helix Magazine*, 19 Nov. 2012, helix.northwestern.edu. Accessed 1 July 2020.

What's the Big Idea?

Read this quote carefully. What is its main idea? Explain how the main idea is supported by details.

A magnified image shows chloroplasts, *green dots*, in plant cells.

From Sunlight to Sugars

A chloroplast is a structure within the cells of plants. This is where the process of photosynthesis takes place. Chloroplasts contain chlorophyll. This **substance** takes in sunlight. Chlorophyll gives leaves their green color.

Atoms and Molecules

To understand photosynthesis, it's important to know about elements, **atoms**, and **molecules**. An element is a specific type of chemical. An atom is the smallest individual piece of an element. And a molecule is a group of atoms that combine to create a substance.

Leaf Colors

Leaves have other colors besides green. But these colors may only be visible in the fall. The air is cooler. Leaves stop photosynthesizing. The green chlorophyll breaks down. Yellow and orange colors in the leaves become visible in some, while other leaves may develop red colors.

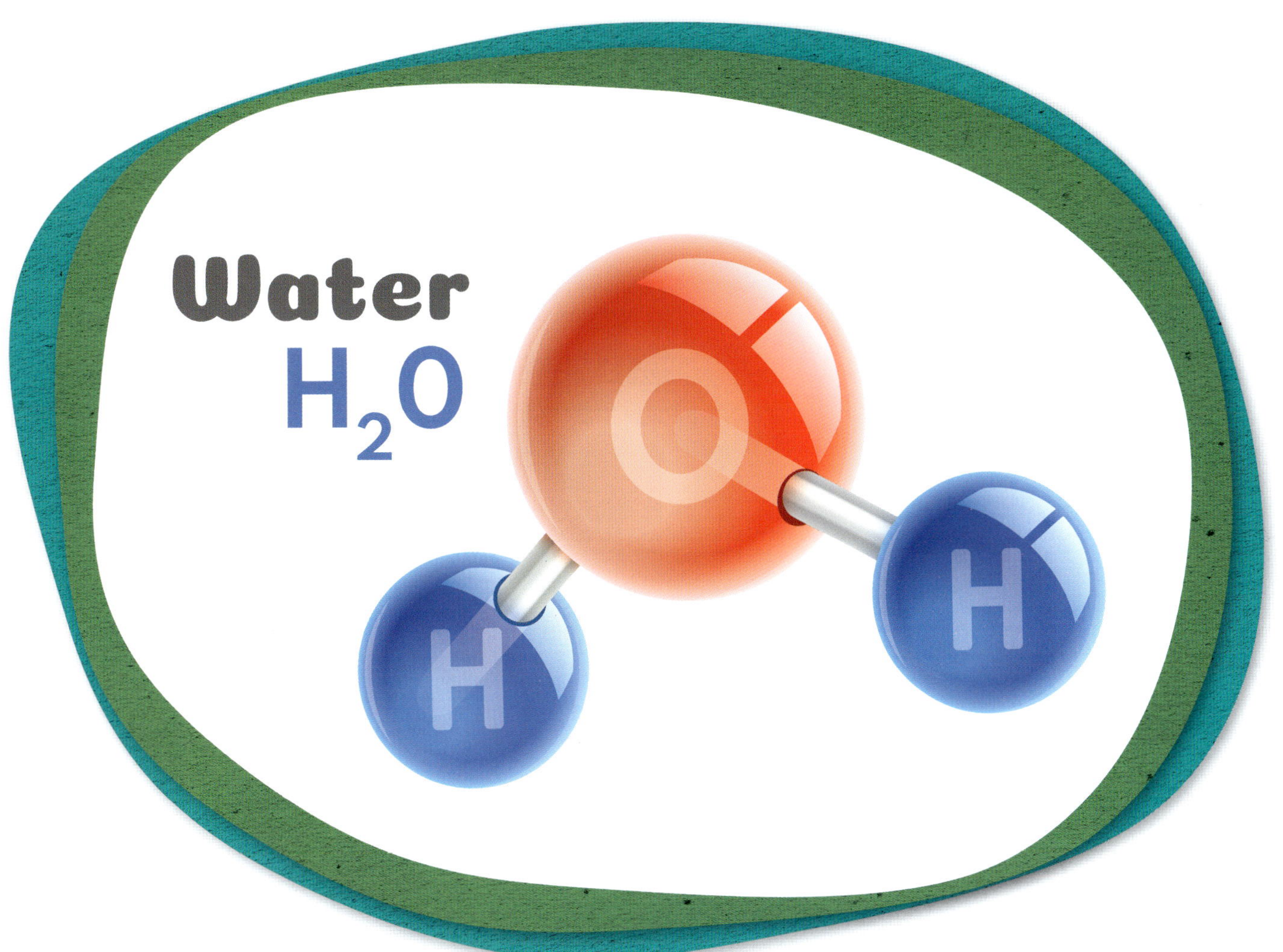

A water molecule is also called H_2O. That is because it has two hydrogen atoms and one oxygen atom.

Water molecules are made up of two hydrogen atoms and one oxygen atom. Carbon dioxide molecules are made up of one carbon atom and two oxygen atoms.

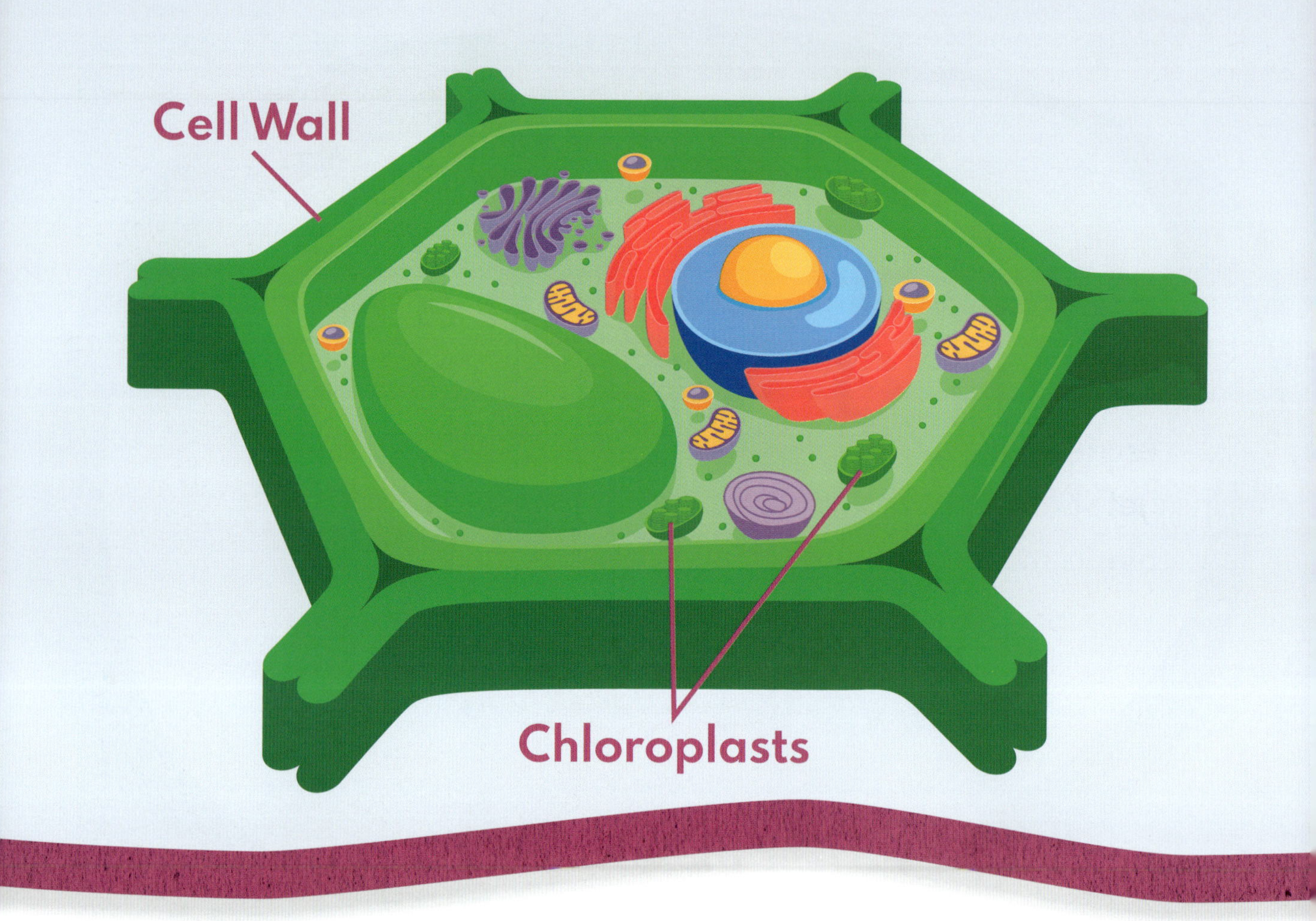

The cell wall and chloroplasts are just two of the many important structures in a plant cell.

Rearranging Atoms

Plants use light energy captured by chlorophyll to split water into two hydrogen atoms and an oxygen atom. The oxygen atom joins with a second oxygen atom after a second water

Animals can eat plants to get some of the sugars the plants made.

molecule is split. The two joined atoms of oxygen form the oxygen gas that humans need to breathe. Humans and other animals need oxygen in order to use the energy in sugars that they eat. Plants also need oxygen to use the energy in the sugars that they make.

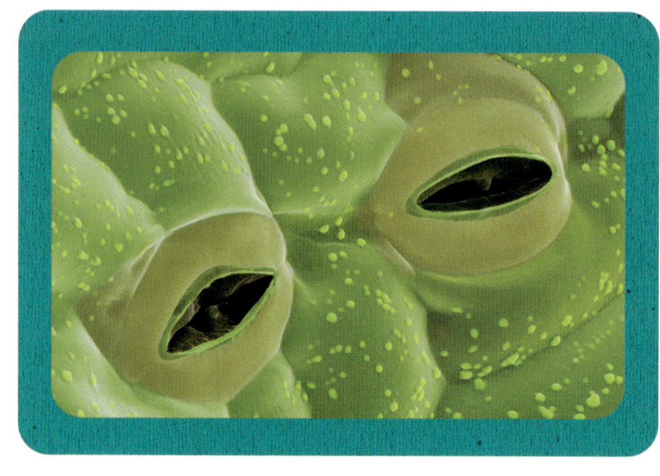

The stomata in leaves can open to allow carbon dioxide in.

When water is split, this releases and energizes two small particles called electrons. These energized electrons combine with carbon and oxygen atoms from carbon dioxide and hydrogen atoms from water. They form a molecule of glucose. Glucose is a type of sugar. Each glucose molecule has six carbon atoms, six oxygen atoms, and 12 hydrogen atoms. Plant cells use the molecules of sugar to get the energy they need to stay alive and grow. Animals can eat the plants and use these sugars for energy too.

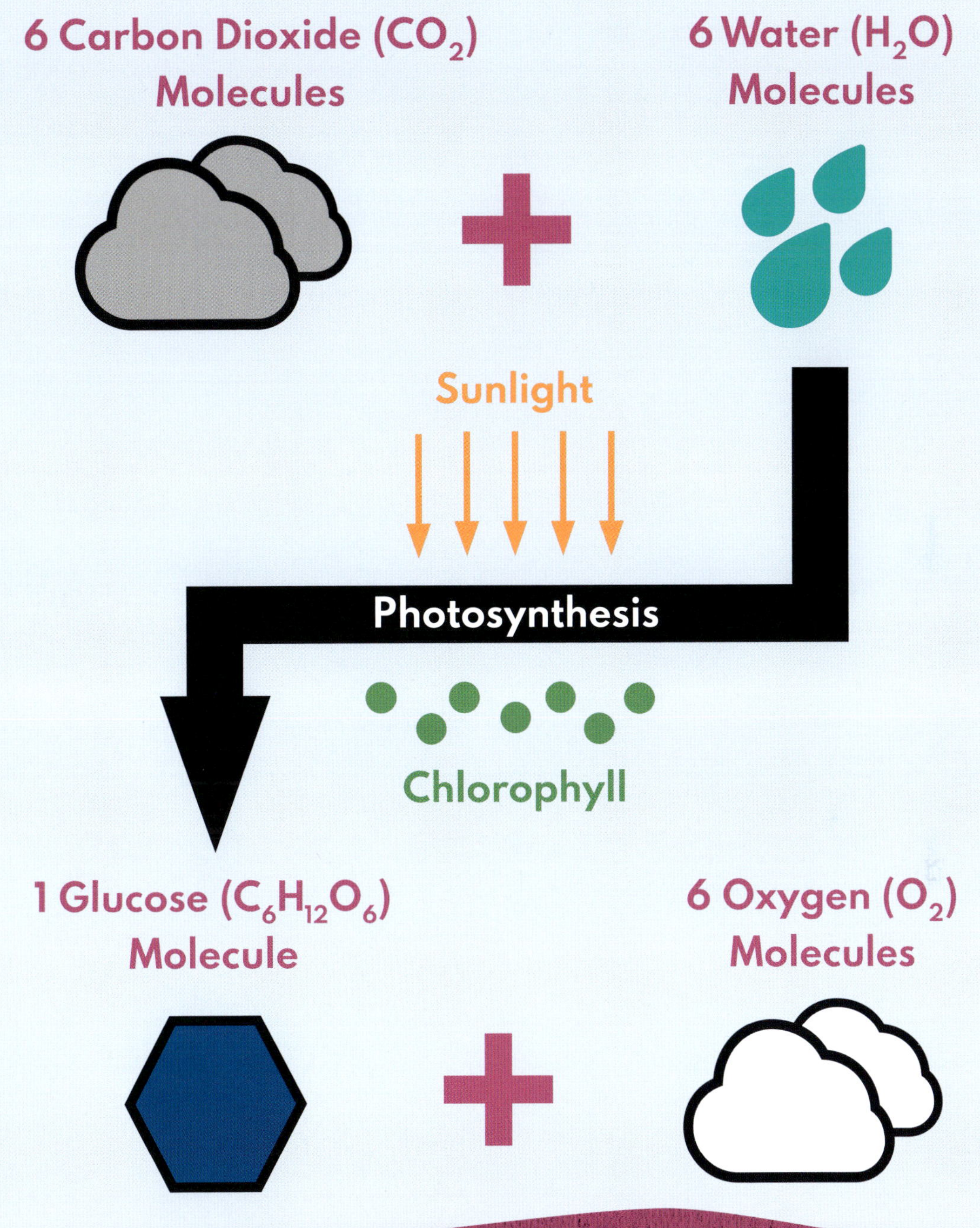

This image shows the photosynthesis equation, which is explained in this chapter.

Photosynthesis gives plants the energy they need to grow and reproduce.

Energy to Grow

Cells store the energy made by photosynthesis. They can use it to divide into two new cells. As cells divide, plants grow. Plants also use energy to grow flowers or fruits. Seeds form. When seeds drop to the soil, some of them sprout. The process of photosynthesis begins again.

Further Evidence

Look at the website below. Does it give any new evidence to support Chapter Three?

How Plants Make Food

abdocorelibrary.com/photosynthesis

Picture Biology

- Plants use carbon dioxide, water, and sunlight to make energy the plant can use. That energy is a kind of sugar called glucose.
- Plants release extra oxygen into the air. Humans and other animals breathe that oxygen.

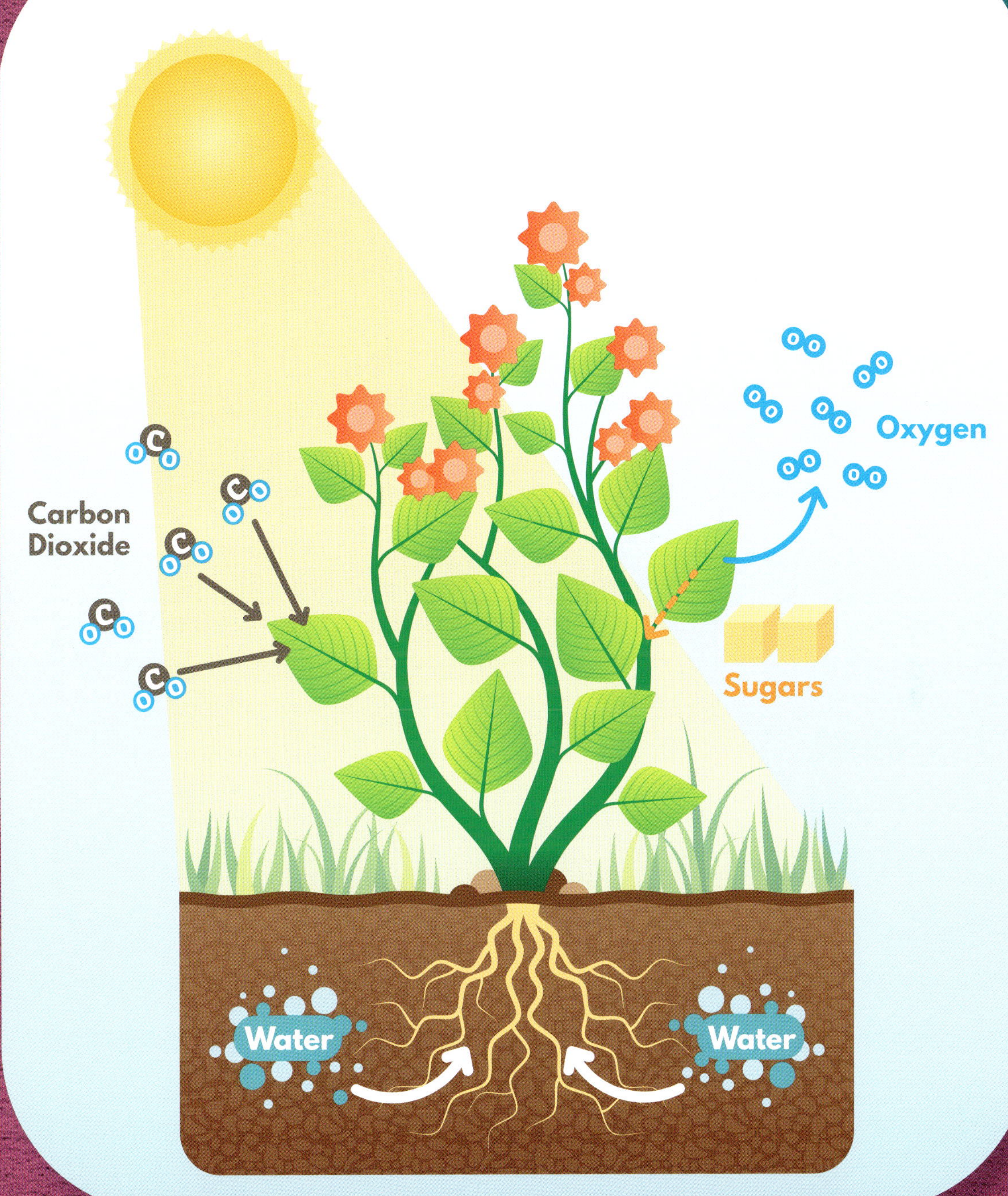
PHOTOSYNTHESIS
Carbon Dioxide
Oxygen
Sugars
Water
Water

Glossary

adapted
changed as a species in order to survive in a certain place

atoms
the smallest individual pieces of a substance

cells
the simplest units of life

molecules
groups of atoms that make up a substance

nutrients
substances and other ingredients that plants and animals need to be healthy

substance
matter, such as a solid, liquid, or gas

Online Resources

To learn more about photosynthesis, visit our free resource websites below.

Visit **abdocorelibrary.com** or scan this QR code for free Common Core resources for teachers and students, including vetted activities, multimedia, and booklinks, for deeper subject comprehension.

Visit **abdobooklinks.com** or scan this QR code for free additional online weblinks for further learning. These links are routinely monitored and updated to provide the most current information available.

Learn More

Bullard, Lisa. *Plants*. Abdo Publishing, 2020.

London, Martha. *Cells*. Abdo Publishing, 2022.

Peterson, Christine. *Study Soils*. Abdo Publishing, 2020.

Index

About the Author

Martha London lives and works in Minnesota. She writes books for young readers full-time. When Martha isn't writing books, you can find her hiking in the woods or snuggled up with her cat.